NIETZSCHE

FOR BEGINNERS

MARC SAUTET

ILLUSTRATED BY PATRICK BOUSSIGNAC

Writers and Readers

WRITERS AND READERS PUBLISHING, INCORPORATED
P.O. Box 461 Village Station
New York, New York 10014

A Writers and Readers Documentary Comic Book
Copyright © 1990

ISBN 0 86316 118 9
0 9 8 7 6 5 4 3 2 1

Manufactured in the United States of America

Beginners Documentary Comic books are published by
Writers and Readers Publishing, Inc. Its trademark, consisting
of the words "For Beginners, Writers and Readers Documentary Comic Books" and Writers and Readers logo, is registered
in the U.S. Patent and Trademark Office and in other
countries.

**Why do I know a few
things more?
Why am I altogether so clever? I
have never reflected on
questions that are none . . .**

	In Europe	The Stars
1848	revolution!	Hegel
1864	the First International	
1866	Prussia attacks Austria	
1869	worker's strikes	Schopenhauer
1870	Germany crushes France	Strauss
1871	the Commune!	
1872	worker's strikes	
	Bismarck against the Catholic Church	
1873	Vienna crash	
	threat of war	
	German socialists unite at Gotha	
1877	Russia attacks Turkey	Clausius,
1878	Bismarck attacks the social democrats	Wagner
1881	the nihilists assassinate the Tsar	
	the socialists call an election	Darwin
	victory for the liberals	
1887	will Austria wage war on Russia?	Renan
	world war	
1888	death of Wulhelm I	
1889	fresh strikes	
	foundation of the Second International	
1890	Bismarck's resignation	
		Nietzsche
1900	war or revolution?	

1st movement

riedrich Nietzsche was born in Röcken near Leipzig in Saxony on 15 October 1844.

If we are to believe his grandmother, the Nietzsches were descended from . . .

What we *do* know is that five generations of Nietzsche's family produced 20 clergymen!

The NIETZKYS members of the Polish aristocracy!
So what? I'll believe it if I want to!

His paternal grandfather, Friedrich August Ludwig (1756–1826), was an outstanding preacher . . .

In 1796 Nietzsche's grandfather was granted an honorary doctorate by the University of Königsberg for his defence of Christianity (*Gamaliel*), written in an attempt to calm the spiritual unrest caused by the French Revolution.

His father, Karl Ludwig (1813–1849), was also a pastor and tutor to the Duke of Saxony's daughters. His parish had been given to him by the King of Prussia, Friedrich Wilhelm IV himself. But, alas! . . .

My father was traumatized by the Revolution of 1848.

Was this trauma fatal? . . . He died a year later.

The son, whom he had adored, was heartbroken. From that moment on the young Nietzsche kept up a serious and dignified exterior, as if he had received a particularly lofty mission in life . . .

N.B. This analysis is entirely the work of the author. It was not even dreamt of by Freud!

1854 The King of Prussia visited Naumburg, where Nietzsche's family now lived.

Fritz, who had become very religious, now had a chance to show his affection for Friedrich Wilhelm IV, whom he had admired since the Revolution of 1848. Friedrich Wilhelm was a feudalistic king, appalled by the concept of democracy and by modern ideas.

1855 The Tsar of Russia had plans for conquering Constantinople, the upshot of which was the Crimean War. The Russians were besieged at Sebastopol by the French and the English, who came to the aid of the Turks.

At college, Fritz developed a political consciousness.

In October 1858 Fritz won a scholarship to Schulpforta, a school for the children of the élite, which had a total of 200 pupils. The standard was high, and as for discipline . . .

Schulpforta, 13

Dear Mommy,
The discipline has been a bit tough this term!

The young Nietzsche worked hard and got good results . . .

But, he's got secret interests!

He's looking his German roots, for one thing!

His scholarship was originally given to him for him to study theology at university and train for the priesthood.

. . . after his school-leaving exams.

It was the path chosen for him by his young, pretty and very religious mother, Franziska, an exceptionally strong-willed woman, and by his younger sister, Elisabeth, known as 'Lama.'

However, Satan was also very interested in young Fritz's career, judging from the company he kept at the age of 18!

* Every month, all the members of the group had to submit:
  – an essay, a poem, or a musical composition
  – a contribution towards the cost of books, musical scores, etc.

17

Who was to win the battle for his soul, the Devil or God?

THE TOUR OF THE NIETZSCHE MUSEUM BEGINS: *1. In 1864 he sailed through his school-leaving exams. 2. Nietzsche enrolled in Theology at the University of Bonn. 3. . . . and in* Philology.* *4. Nietzsche with his Franconian friends. 5. Nietzsche singing in the University choir.*

* Study of literature, e.g. ancient Greek and Latin.

*6. Nietzsche left Bonn. . . for Leipzig.
7. Nietzsche went to Professor Ritschl's inaugural lesson. 8. Nietzsche became great friends with Erwin Rohde. 9. Nietzsche gave up Theology!*

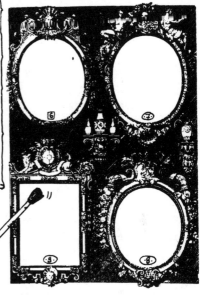

God spare us!

Then began for Nietzsche a period of frenetically studying the Greeks (Theognis, Suidas and Hesiod, in particular), the problems of their authenticity and the links between their works. *

But excursions into town diverted him from the prescribed path.

* A definition of philology worth remembering.

* and Greek

Having no answer to this question, Fritz began feverishly reading philosophy.

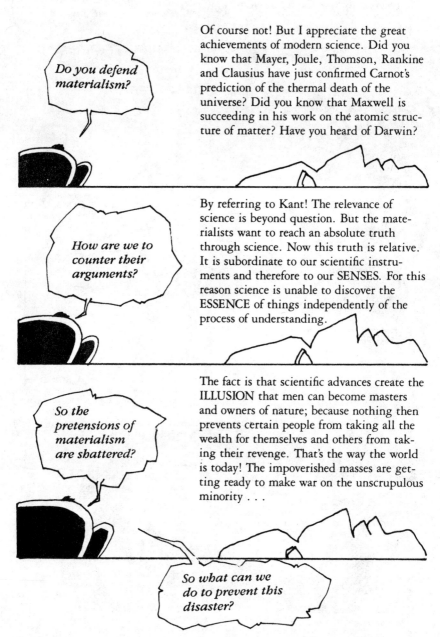

Do you defend materialism?

Of course not! But I appreciate the great achievements of modern science. Did you know that Mayer, Joule, Thomson, Rankine and Clausius have just confirmed Carnot's prediction of the thermal death of the universe? Did you know that Maxwell is succeeding in his work on the atomic structure of matter? Have you heard of Darwin?

How are we to counter their arguments?

By referring to Kant! The relevance of science is beyond question. But the materialists want to reach an absolute truth through science. Now this truth is relative. It is subordinate to our scientific instruments and therefore to our SENSES. For this reason science is unable to discover the ESSENCE of things independently of the process of understanding.

So the pretensions of materialism are shattered?

The fact is that scientific advances create the ILLUSION that men can become masters and owners of nature; because nothing then prevents certain people from taking all the wealth for themselves and others from taking their revenge. That's the way the world is today! The impoverished masses are getting ready to make war on the unscrupulous minority . . .

So what can we do to prevent this disaster?

Why have you remained so long in obscurity?

Because I had to wait for that good-for-nothing Hegel to be discredited. Hegel blinded whole generations with his IDEALISM. He had the idea that when Man thinks, it is Nature which is thinking itself! Nothing more tempting for the golden boy of our time: to be the BEING . . .

But did you say anything Kant didn't say?

Yes and no! I defended Kant against Hegel's attempts to outdo him. And I insist that Kant is unsurpassed in his criticism of the powers of human reason. Reason enables man to conceive of the universe but his senses prevent him from doing so. To establish universal laws one must go beyond all possible experience. In other words, Science takes its laws from Reason and not from Being. The objectivity of knowledge is just a myth.

Then where do you disagree with him?

Deep down Kant is still an optimist. He still accepts the objective existence of things, of Being. And since he had nothing to say about it, he let Hegel speak. He just missed the truth. The truth is that everything that lives, suffers. There you have the ESSENCE of existence. Why this suffering? Because there is WANT: to live is to want, to want is to suffer. If there is a curse on man, it is that!!!

Is there no redemption?

In 1866 the Germans caught political fever.

In the formation of modern nations, Germany was lagging behind. It was made up of small states, independent of one another and subject to Austria. It did NOT EXIST!

Our right is the right of the German nation to exist, to breathe and to unite itself.

It is the duty of Prussia to give the German nation the necessary basis for its existence.

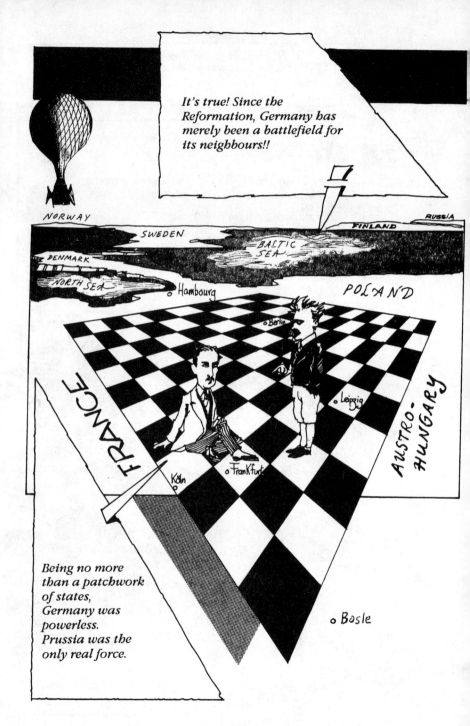

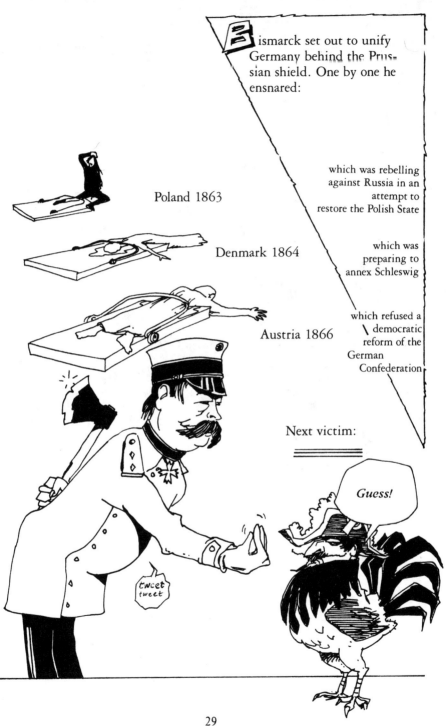

Bismarck set out to unify Germany behind the Prussian shield. One by one he ensnared:

Poland 1863

which was rebelling against Russia in an attempt to restore the Polish State

Denmark 1864

which was preparing to annex Schleswig

Austria 1866

which refused a democratic reform of the German Confederation

Next victim:

Guess!

tweet tweet

In October 1867 military service offered Fritz an escape from the pedantry and laboured erudition of university work.

France was an obstacle to German unification. In 1870 Napoleon vetoed the accession of a German prince to the Spanish throne and this resulted in . . .

Meanwhile, Fritz was not called up.

In July he went on his first holiday in the Alps! But he soon asked for university leave. After a brief medical training he went to the front.

. . . to transport supplies . . .

. . . and casualties . . .

Duty to Germany comes first!

NIETZSCHE AFTER THE BATTLE OF WOERTH.

... Yesterday one million men lost, today 100,000.

Direction : Nancy. Hotel Dombasle. Soldiers in the market. Spy. Dirt.

Direction: Ars, South Mos

Paris was shelled throughout the winter!

Proclamation of the German Empire at Versailles!

Fritz was repatriated after catching diphtheria. After a few weeks' convalescence he took up his post again at Basle.

HE'S YOUNG. HE'S GOT HIS WHOLE FUTURE AHEAD OF HIM.

2 nd movement

His first book is on its way!

The Birth of Tragedy

Nietzsche was 27 years old when his first book appeared in 1872. In it he proposed a solution to an enigma that had long been puzzling philologists: the origins of Greek tragedy, of which Aeschylus, Sophocles and Euripedes were the supreme exponents.

This book corresponds to what he had learnt at
UNIVERSITY   and at   SCHOOL

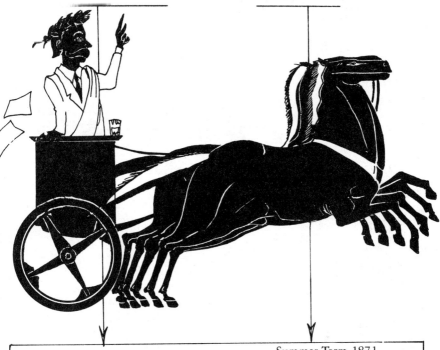

Winter Term 1870–1871	Summer Term 1871
	● Introduction to the study of classical philology
● History of the Greek epic	● Quintilian, Book 1
● Greek metric	● Sophocles, *Oedipus rex*
● Hesiod, *Works and Days*	● Hesiod, *Works and Days*
● Quintilian, Book 1	● Principal forms of poetry, with examples:
● Cicero, *Academica*	– epic poetry, Hesiod, *Works*
● Plato, *Phaedon*	– elegy, Tyrtaios, Solon, Simonides, Pindar
	– bucolic poetry, Theocritus
	– drama, Aeschylus, *Prometheus*

Winter Term 1871–1872
● Introduction to the study of Platonic dialogue
● Dialogus, *De oratoribus*
● Latin epigraphy
● Hesiod
● Principal forms of Greek poetry:
– Plato, *Phaedon*
– Demosthenes, *Philippika* 1 & 2

● Other reading:

Heroditus Thucydides, Plato,
Demosthenes, Plutarch, Lucian,
Homer, Aeschylus,
Euripides, Aristophanes

WHERE IS THE ENIGMA?

We have no problem in agreeing that:

1. Tragedy was initially the celebration of the god Dionysus.
2. This celebration first took the form of a dancing and singing procession (the dithyramb).
3. This chorus of dancing and singing actors was the origin of drama.

After his nomination as a full Ordinary Professor, Fritz came up with an extraordinary solution!

According to Kant, Being is the very essence of things. It is reality independently of the way in which things appear to us:

I call it the 'thing in itself.' I differentiate it from phenomena, that is, the world as it appears to us.

You've forgotten him!

Emmanuel Kant
Philosopher at Königsberg
(1724-1804)

Human reason . . . is burdened by questions which, as prescribed by the very nature of reason itself, it is not able to ignore, but which, as transcending all its powers, it is also not able to answer. (*Critique of Pure Reason*, 1781)

Schopenhauer radicalized Kant's epistemological pessimism, and he had a good point: the rest of us, like all living beings, are on the side of appearances. . .

. . . which accounts for our sufferings. We are fugitives, doomed to sickness, nostalgia and death. Because we are only moments in a process which continues after our destruction. . .

* Don't panic: there's a glossary at the end of this book!!!

Tragedy transforms the human condition:
—the songs and dances of the chorus reveal the cruelty of Being
—the spectators enjoy what takes place on the stage and therefore
 accept this revelation.

Any advance on this? Nietzsche goes on to tackle the counter-proof by answering a connected question: why did Greek tragedy disappear so quickly?

Why?
Because the music was taken out of it!
1. Dialogue replaced music.
2. The hero replaced the chorus.
And when the music disappeared the irrational truth of the human condition was obscured. Tragedy then lost its point.

Euripides playwright—480—406

Euripides was to blame for this rapid decline!

It was at the time of the wars in the 5th century that tragedy reached its peak.

Under threat from the Persians, the Greeks had to choose between two evils: 1. Militarism 2. Defeat They needed instant remedy—tragedy provided it.

INDICATIONS

1. Nationalist fever (deification of the State, the nation and the fatherland)
2. Revolutionary intoxication (rejection of the State, the nation and the fatherland, and of exploitation) . . .
   . . . and sexual debauchery.

Tragedy is "medication".

The two dangers were:
1. An excess of Apollinism (Apollo = god of the State).
2. An excess of Dionysianism (Dionysus = god of the oppressed).

Yes, it's true, Attic tragedy reached its peak at the time of the Persian Wars. It's convincing. But how did you make this discovery?

Simple! By observing our present situation. We've just been at war too . . .

. . . Yes! Against the French!

We too have experienced the Apolline peril . . .

You are thinking of Prussian imperialism.

We know what the Dionysian peril is like too. . .

The INTERNATIONAL!! !!

And look what came out of this atmosphere of conflict.

The Musical Drama of

Richard Wagner

49

WE'VE GOT:
The imperialist threat.

The Birth of Tragedy establishes a parallel between:
—the victory of the Greeks over the Persians
—the victory of the Germans over the French.

18 January 1871. Proclamation of the German Empire at Versailles.

And we've got: the revolutionary threat

The Birth of Tragedy also draws a parallel between:
—the cult of Dionysus in Greece.
—the revolutionary sweep in Europe.

> Gentlemen, you may think the Commune's aspirations are wrong, even mad, but you can be sure that the whole European proletariat is on the side of Paris!

BEBEL (1840–1913) Socialist deputy Speech of 25 May 1871 at the Reichstag

28 March 1871 Proclamation of the Commune!

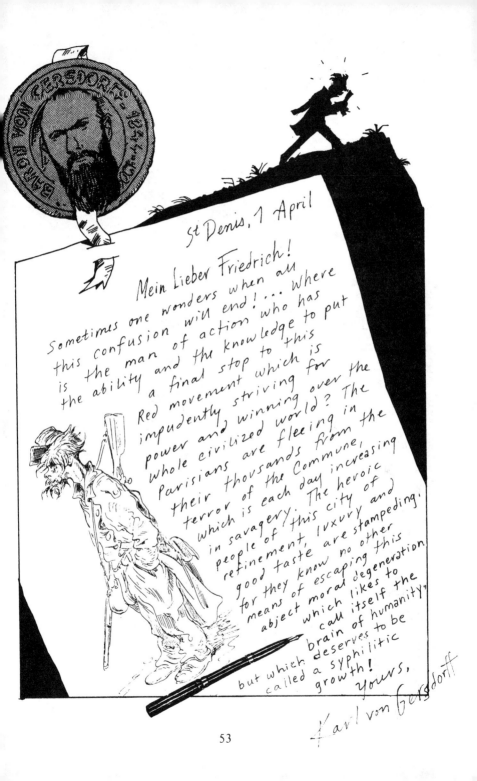

St Denis, 1 April

Mein Lieber Friedrich!

Sometimes one wonders when all this confusion will end! ... Where is the man of action who has the ability and the knowledge to put a final stop to this Red movement which is impudently striving for power and winning over the whole civilized world? The Parisians are fleeing from their thousands from the terror of the Commune, which is each day increasing in savagery. The heroic people of this city of refinement, luxury and good taste are stampeding, for they know no other means of escaping this abject moral degeneration which likes to call itself the brain of humanity, but which deserves to be called a syphilitic growth!

Yours,

Karl von Gersdorff

53

So, like the 5th-century Greeks, we are forced to make a difficult choice, and, like the Greeks . . .

.. WE HAVE ...

... our Aeschylus:

Wagner

... the genius of music drama!

Why, I'm fighting to ward
them off, of course!. . .

. . . why would I have written this book
if not to warn my contemporaries of
the impending catastrophe. . .

. . . And to show that only
WAGNER can save us!!!

WAGNER?

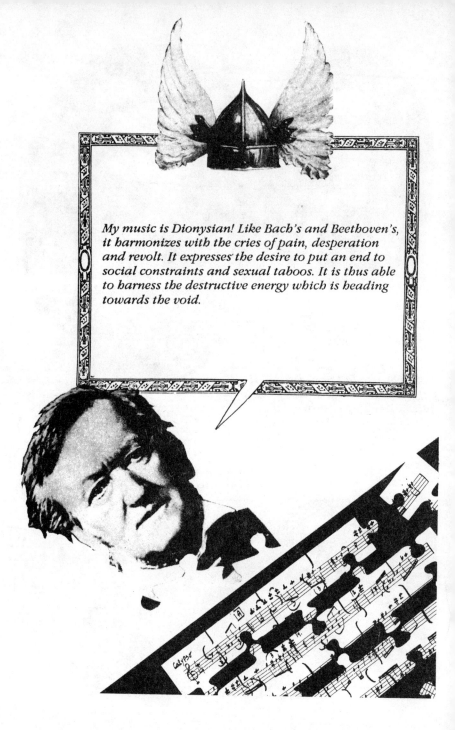

*My music is Dionysian! Like Bach's and Beethoven's,
it harmonizes with the cries of pain, desperation
and revolt. It expresses the desire to put an end to
social constraints and sexual taboos. It is thus able
to harness the destructive energy which is heading
towards the void.*

MUSIC

My drama is Appolline! What happens on stage gives pleasure to the audience, because the heroes take on its suffering. The suffering then becomes enjoyment.

But I thought you were a revolutionary, Mr. Wagner?

In 1871 Wagner still enjoyed the reputation of being a revolutionary because:
1. He had taken part in the revolution of 1848 (in Dresden).
2. He had written statements in favour of the abolition of exploitation (*Art and Revolution*).
3. He described his art as the 'art of the future'.

BUT HE IS NO LONGER REVOLUTIONARY! For a long time now he has been a pessimist! Since 1854 he's been a disciple of Schopenhauer!...

In *The Ring of the Nibelung* I accepted the truth of human affairs. Everything is tragic and the Will which sought to create a world according to its wishes could only find true satisfaction finally in the dignity of being buried under its own ruins.

Did you hear that? "The Will which sought to create a world according to its wishes..."

In 1871 Wagner condemned the predominant spirit of the Italian Renaissance in the modern world

Like Palastrina's music, religion had disappeared from the church. We know that it was the German spirit (so feared and hated 'beyond the mountains') which everywhere and equally in the sphere of Art opposed this spiritual corruption of the peoples of Europe — for the sake of their own salvation.

Wagner was not alone in renouncing optimism.

> *If you think you can rejoice in the disappearance of the German spirit, listen to this!*

> *I must admit modern culture is heading towards a crises!*

Jacob Burckhardt

In his *Civilization of the Renaissance in Italy,* Burckhardt welcomed the emergence of the Philosophes. But in 1870–1871, in his lectures on *Universal History,* he deplored the consequences.

The upshot was that Nietzsche
saw the prophecy of Engels and
Marx come true:
'The bourgeoisie produces . . .
its own gravediggers.'
From now on, the workers want
paradise on earth.
The dominant classes are heading towards catastrophe.

'If it's true that the Greeks perished from slavery, it is equally true that we will die from lack of slavery. The vast majority must be subjected to a life in the service of the minority and beyond the limited needs of its own existence.'

So this nut case wants the exploited to resign themselves to their fate!

... and that the exploiters stop being optimistic! And so the veil which hides the cruelty of things will be removed!

Beyond the international conflicts, a dismayed Nietzsche saw the German proletariat take up the banner of the Communards:

'Beyond the struggle between nations, we were suddenly shocked by the terrible appearance of the international hydra, heralding struggles of a very different kind in the future.'

'There is nothing more terrible than a class of barbaric slaves who have learned to regard their existence as an injustice, and now prepare to avenge, not only themselves, but all generations.'

INSTITUTIONALIZE
WE MUST *WAGNERIAN DRAMA!*

The pleasure obtained from the spectacle transforms society. What the Greeks achieved through Aeschylus, the Germans can get from me. . .

In short:

DIONYSIAN MUSIC +
APOLLINE DRAMA
= OPIUM OF THE PEOPLE

Opium, that's clever! All our casualties have been given morphine since 1870!

With Nietzsche's *Birth of Tragedy* Nietzsche and Wagner joined forces in order to persuade Bismarck to agree to the Reich financing the Bayreuth theatre and its productions.

How successful was <u>The Birth of Tragedy</u>?

It scandalized most university philologists. A young Berlin aristocrat became their spokesman.

1. *You defend Wagner.*
2. *You make Apollo political.*
3. *You uproot Dionysus.*
4. *You invent things about Greek music.*
5. *You make Socrates older than Euripedes.*
6. *You criticize Euripedes. You are a disgrace to the profession! And since Schopenhauer suggests you resign, resign you shall!*

Huh! Fancy coming from such a good family and speaking on behalf of Berlin Jewry!

Ulrich von Willamowitz-Moellendorf
philologist 1848-1931

Despite everything, the book was a success with the nobility.

71

It was from this battle that Nietzsche's second book resulted: the first of his *Untimely Meditations* (August 1873). By attacking Friedrich David Strauss, Fritz sought to strike a blow at 'the cultivated philistines', that is, the incorrigible optimists!

Nietzsche published the second volume of *Untimely Meditations* in February 1874. Wilamowitz claimed to be able to teach him the proper way to use history; Nietzsche therefore analysed the advantages and disadvantages of history, in 'On the Uses of History.'

He maintained that history can impart courage just as easily as it can paralyze. Now, there is one particularly harmful form of this paralysis which (like Strauss's optimism) is very popular:
'the surrender to the process of universal history' advocated by:

Edouard von Hartmann
philosopher of the unconscious (1842-1906)

In 1869 *Philosophy of the Unconscious* appeared in its fourth edition (6,000 copies sold in three years).

Rogue! Scoundrel! That's giving in to socialism!

The third volume of *Untimely Meditations*, 'Schopenhauer as Educator', published in October 1874, is less aggressive. Nietzsche seems less convinced that he will succeed in making his point.

'We live in the age of atoms, in an atomistic chaos. In the Middle Ages the opposing forces were held together by the Church, to some extent assimilated into each other under the strong pressure it exerted. Since this pressure has diminished the opposing forces have rebelled against each other . . . We are now being swept along by the ice-filled torrent of the Middle Ages; the thaw is over and a powerful and devastating movement is developing. Ice-floe piles up on ice-floe and all the banks have been inundated and are in danger of collapse. Nothing can hold back the revolution—the atomic revolution.'

In this maze, the only guide left is Schopenhauer.

1874 CRISIS!

DIPLOMATIC CRISIS IN EUROPE

1. France had rearmed
2. Russia had its eye on the Balkans
—How could Germany avoid war?

ECONOMIC CRISIS

1. Financial crash in Vienna
2. Banks collapsing
3. Industries collapsing
—How would the workers react?

NIETZSCHE IN CRISIS

1. Finance for Bayreuth dried up
2. Bismarck was reluctant to help out
—How could Wagner succeed?

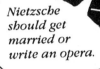

Nietzsche should get married or write an opera.

a) Wagner had the misfortune of brushing with the King of Bavaria, Louis II. All the King's eccentricities were now blamed on him!

b) Through his earlier, compromising connection with the Revolution of 1848, he had lost all his potential patrons!

c) In the eyes of the socialists he was a traitor.

d) Finally, he upset the Jews with his pamphlet *Judaism in Music*!

After many setbacks, the Bayreuth theatre was finally completed in 1876. Nietzsche wrote a defence of Wagner in his fourth volume of *Untimely Meditations*: 'Richard Wagner in Bayreuth.'

'To subdue contending masses to a simple rhythm, to subject a multiplicity of demands and desires to the rule of a single will—these are the tasks for which (Wagner) feels he was born.'

The festival had begun! <u>The Ring of the Nibelung</u> would be performed for the first time!

Ask for the
programme!

13 August: *The Rhine
Gold*
14 August: *The
Walkyrie*
15 August: Rest!
16 August: *Siegfried*
17 August: Götter-
dämmerung (*Twilight of
the Gods*)

Present:
Pedro II, Emperor of
Brazil, the King of
Würtemberg, Grand-
Duke Karl Alexander
of Saxony-Weimar, sev-
eral princes, Baroness
von Schleinitz, Anton
Bruckner, Piotr Ilitch
Tchaikovsky, Ludwig
Scheman, Henry
Thode, the Wesen-
donks, Mathilde Maïer,
Prof. Dr. Nietzsche.

Absent:
Louis II of Bavaria,
and . . .
. . . the working class.

*Nietzsche's
there.*

*Nietzsche's
tired.*

*Nietzsche's
tied up.*

78

WHAT IS <u>THE RING OF NIBELUNG</u> ABOUT?

Wagner has always used German legends. In *The Ring*, he puts me, Wotan, head of the Gods, on stage. My power is weakened by the contract I've made with the Giants who built my castle, Valhalla, home of the Gods. In return, I've had to get for them the ring, forged from Rhine Gold, which belonged to the Nibelung. That's bad news. And I need Siegfried to get the ring back . . .

But there's a curse on this ring! It brings the downfall of whoever possesses it. How will it all end?

Disastrously!

How will the story be presented?

As a series of three complete Greek tragedies, preceded by a shorter prelude. The music is more important than in opera, but the orchestra isn't visible. The audience is seated in tiered seats.

When is it going to be performed?

The festival takes place only once a year, and . . . most important . . . *The Ring* must only be performed at Bayreuth!

Nietzsche was terribly disappointed and used his extremely bad headaches as a pretext for escaping the Festival.

shortly after

Malwida von Meysenbug

a friend of Wagner, invited Nietzsche to her house in Naples.

Like Wagner (and lots of others) I've moved on from socialist optimism to Schopenhaurian pessimism: you'll be at home here!

AM IN A BAD WAY –stop– LEAVE GRANTED BY UNIVERSITY– stop– ARRIVING IMMEDIATELY –stop–
NIETZSCHE

He was accompanied on his Italian trip by Paul Rée (a philosophy student at Basle University) who was writing a book on *The Origin of the Moral Sensations*.

The trip was a turning point! Nietzsche was about to reassess the years he had spent defending Wagner:

Nietzsche met Wagner again at Sorrento.

1. The Reich refuses to support the Festival.
2. There are debts of 148,000 gold marks!
3. Attendance was poor
4. The show was pathetic!

3 ʳᵈ movement

Piano.

But if there's no hope in Germany or
Wagner, where will we find our salvation?...

Nietzsche wondered what had made him defend Wagner in the past. He examined the value of art; the origin of morals; truth and illusion, and eventually decided that all this was: *Human, All-Too-Human*.

Here comes the little saint! My word! He's running away from the Devil!

.... or else he's on his way to join him!

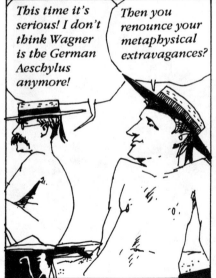

87

As for political dangers, I vouch for: 1. Peace with Russia. 2. War with the socialists.

1878 Bismarck
1. Organized the Berlin congress.
2. Passed anti-socialist laws.

Prohibition of propaganda meetings and the socialist press!

Bismark isn't stupid. If war breaks out and Russia no longer polices Europe, then we'll be dangerous.

A. Wagner was also despairing over modern Germany and took refuge in his new work: *Parsifal*.

The libretto was finished at the end of 1877.
The story, which takes place one Easter Day,
revolves round the mystery of the Eucharist.
Parsifal realizes that it is his mission to save the
world using the chalice which held the blood of
Christ—the Grail.

Nietzsche had every reason therefore to continue his rationalist cure!

Wieder sehen!! My health has forced me to give up teaching. I'm leaving Basle for a better climate.

So in 1879
Assorted Opinions and Maxims
'against illusion' appeared.

Soon the Wanderer is hailed by the Shadow.

1880

THE WANDERER
AND
HIS SHADOW

I HAVEN'T HEARD YOU SPEAK FOR A LONG TIME.

But I'm spoken to.

... And continues on the subject of morals.

The criminal and the powerful man who promises a community that he will protect it from the criminal. . .

. . . are probably the same kind of people!

At the start, the community is the organization of the weak!. . .

. . . whose purpose is to curtail the threat of the powerful.

... AND OF MODERN SOCIETY.

1881. In the French moralist tradition *Aurora* digs ever deeper . . .

Chamfort Nicolas Sébastien Roch
(1741–1794)
Thoughts, Maxims, Anecdotes

Vauvenargues
Luc de Clapiers
Marquis of Vauvenargues
(1715–1747)
Characters and Dialogues

La Rochefoucauld
François
Duke of
(1613–1680)
Reflections or Judgements and Moral Maxims

Morality is hypocrisy!

Morality is a delusion.

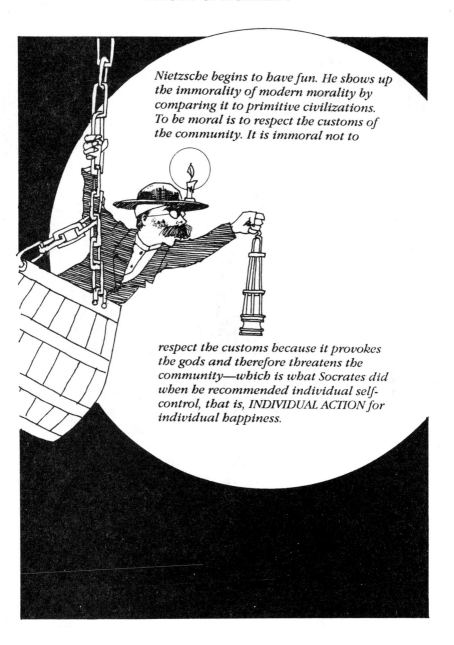

Nietzsche begins to have fun. He shows up the immorality of modern morality by comparing it to primitive civilizations. To be moral is to respect the customs of the community. It is immoral not to

respect the customs because it provokes the gods and therefore threatens the community—which is what Socrates did when he recommended individual self-control, that is, INDIVIDUAL ACTION for individual happiness.

Morality is not specific to man: the whole animal world is moral in that the individual subordinates itself to the group.

98

Christianity, on the other hand, is immoral from the outset because its object is to free the individual from the burden of Jewish tradition. It was hatred of the law (Torah) and his inability to respect it that led Saul to become Paul and invent divine redemption from original sin by exploiting the death of Jesus.

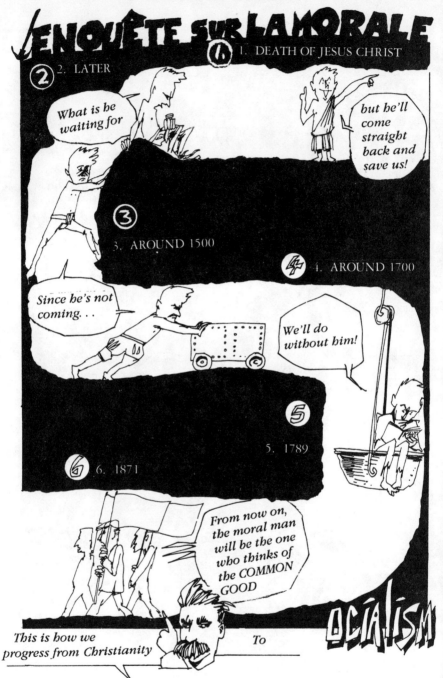

Pity and altruism were once secondary in Christian thinking, but since waiting for the 'end of time' has proved fruitless, they've begun to dominate.

Even if you attach no rational value to the *common good*, you give in to it in fact when you respect *institutions* such as:
– military service
– marriage
– baptism.

When pity and respect for others have become instinctive your *acts* guarantee what your *mind* refuses.

The masses are always more important as a result and eventually seek to subordinate the *State* to their interests and their well-being, regarding them as the purpose of History.

Wählt Bebel

I have great respect for your OPINIONS, but minor nonconformist ACTIONS are worth more!

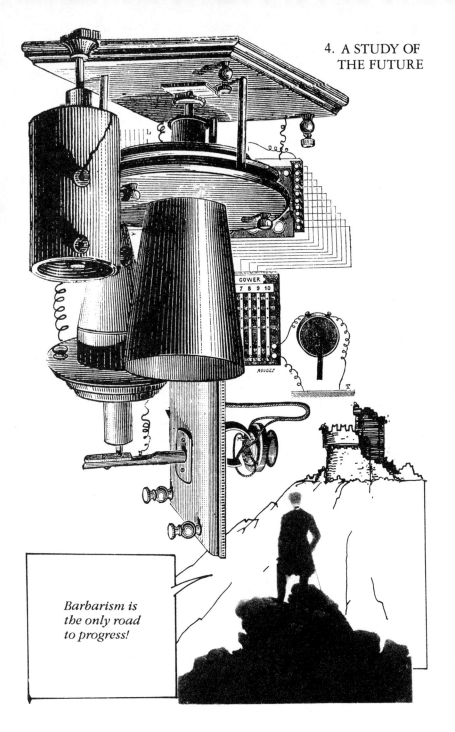

Barbarism is
the only road
to progress!

All these books and research helped Nietzsche to overcome his intellectual and emotional crisis.

Mr. Nietzsche? Oh, he's a lo[t] better! He's become very stoical. He's free and has a small pension from the university. Malwida's right [—] what he needs is to marry [a] rich and beautiful girl!. . .

No. 208: Miss Natalie Herzon.

Not beautiful enough!

No. 209: Miss Elizabeth Brandes.

Not rich enough!

106

Crickey! He's right off the rails!

107

1882

B. Nietzsche lived alone, dividing his time between Saxony and Italy. He had no friends left and no illusions about Germany. While he was taking stock of his new beliefs, Wagner was putting on Parsifal.

He's gone on from opium to hashish!

STATEMENT NO. 1

Man is a rare phenomenon in the vast cosmos which
has no known limits and no recognizable order.
One could accept that life has a meaning if this were
the rule in the cosmos.
But it turns out that life is merely a trivial exception.

STATEMENT NO. 2

The laws of nature are all-too-human inventions.
They are the result of the relationship between man
and what he perceives. Man has need of them even if
they are relative. Therefore, one could say that not
only is there no absolute truth, but that man needs
illusion.

STATEMENT NO. 3

Life, nature and history are totally indifferent to the
meaning which man gives to his actions and his sufferings. 'Original sin' is a good example of the fairy
stories which he invents to mask this indifference.

God is dead!

Science destroys Faith, whereas Christian morality promotes Science.

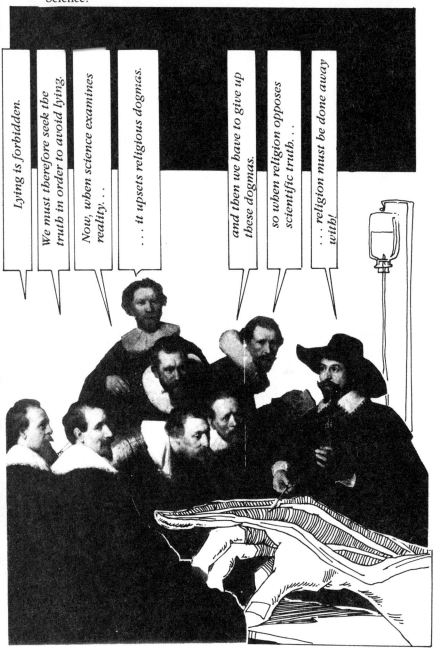

112

A short break, please!
What are the practical consequences of these statements?
And you think that's funny?
Is he showing us a way to live authentically?
Can you spare a dime?
Don't panic! Herr Nietzsche has still got some principles!

PRINCIPLE NO. 1:

to make one's own laws for oneself
because:
like the notions of 'sin' and 'salvation', the notion of 'duty' is an old prejudice which gently suffocates us.

PRINCIPLE NO. 2

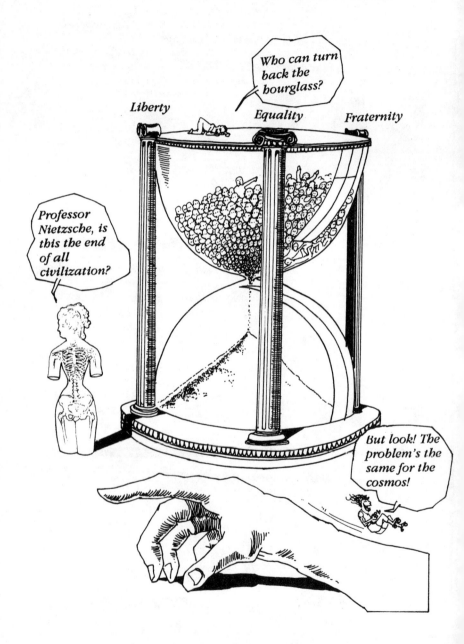

THE QUESTION IS PUT IN TERMS OF HISTORY . . .

If it's true that the modern world tends to level the whole of humanity under a common law, this was also the case in the last years of the Roman Empire.

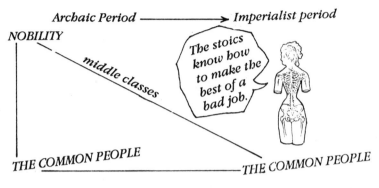

The fall of the Roman Empire didn't lead to the end of History. Does modern democracy mean the end of all civilization?

. . . AND IN COSMOLOGICAL TERMS

If one accepts the theory of the birth of solar systems through condensation of gas and gradual cooling (the Laplace system) and if one accepts the principles of thermodynamics, in particular the degradation of energy (Carnot's second principle) . . .

It remains to be seen if this degradation applies to the whole of the universe and if the death of one system may not lead to the birth of another!

117

ALL OF A SUDDEN! . . .
One day in August 1881
at Sils Maria in Switzer-
land, at 6,000 feet above
sea level:

EVERYTHING RECURS !!!!!......

There you are—he's
found his meta-
physical
consolation! . . .

Hmmph! He's
copying the
Stoics.* Reread
Marcus Aurelius
and Epictetus—it's
the Stoic doctrine
word for word.

* Stoic comes from Stoa, the name of the gateway in Athens around which the Stoics
used to meet.

'Behold this gateway, dwarf! It is the gateway of the moment . . . Two tracks meet there; no one has ever followed them to the end. This long track behind us. It goes on for an eternity. And that long road ahead of us—that is another eternity . . .. But if one were to follow them further and ever further and further: do you think, dwarf, that these roads would be in eternal opposition?"

Does this vision of the Eternal Reccurrence have to be justified scientifically? Should it become a new religion?
It was Nietzsche's friend Ree who persuaded him to test out his theories on the discoveries of thermodynamics . . .

. . . and also Lou von Salome (1861–1937), a beautiful and intelligent Russian girl, whom Malwida had introduced to Fritz and Paul.
Lou was charmed by the two friends and enjoyed spending time with them.

Nietzsche was also captivated; he proposed a trial two-year marriage to Lou.

What could he do? Whose side should he choose? Nietzsche hesitated for several weeks and then cut himself off from his mother and sister. But his friends' doubts about his doctrine, their concern for scientific proofs and their rejection of 'pathos' all isolated him once more . . .

Nietzsche finally gave up and went south, abandoning his friends. He wrote poisoned letters about Rée . . .

4th movement

Vivace.

Emotionally shattered, disillusioned with life and anxious about the future, Nietzsche fell ill once more . . .

and then . . .

At the age of 30, Zarathustra has left home and gone to the mountains . . .

After ten years of solitude he has become very wise.

Confused and disappointed, Zarathustra carries out of the town the body of the tightrope walker, whose fall had been occasioned by the jester while Zarathustra was talking to the crowd.

Zarathustra abandons his efforts to make the crowd wiser. From now on he chooses disciples.

Do not listen to those who preach death. . .

They are the consumptives of the soul—they start dying as soon as they are born!

Having sown the seeds Zarathustra returns to his cave to wait for the harvest.
. . . The years go by.
At last he goes to find his disciples in the Islands of the Blessed . . .
His success and his hardness are assured. He preaches widely . . .

HE PREACHES

AGAINST THE TARAN-TULAS
'You preachers of equality . . . your most secret tyrant-appetite is disguised by your virtuous words.'

IN FAVOUR OF THE SUPER-MAN
'Could you *create* a God?–Then be silent about all Gods! But you could surely create the Superman.'

The star of Zarathustra is ris-
ing. But with it, night falls.

*What weariness with
the present and
nostalgia for the past
I have constantly!...
What does the prophet
say?*

'Everything is empty,
everything is one, everything
is past! All our work has
been in vain, our wine has
become poison!'

I must be alone again! Men only shrink in stature so what good is it to explain the Superman to them? Nothing can stop the victory of NILHILISM?. . .

The vicious circle of eternal recurrence makes Zarathustra ill:

Zarathustra grows old alone. One day he thinks he hears a cry for help.

It's the *higher man*!

He goes in search of him and finds several important people, whom he tells to wait for him in his cave.

When he fails to find what he is looking for, he goes back . . .

The sudden appearance of a lion wakes Zarathustra out of his trance.

Was I dreaming?

For a moment Zarathustra is seized by the desire to save the higher man. But what is left of him?

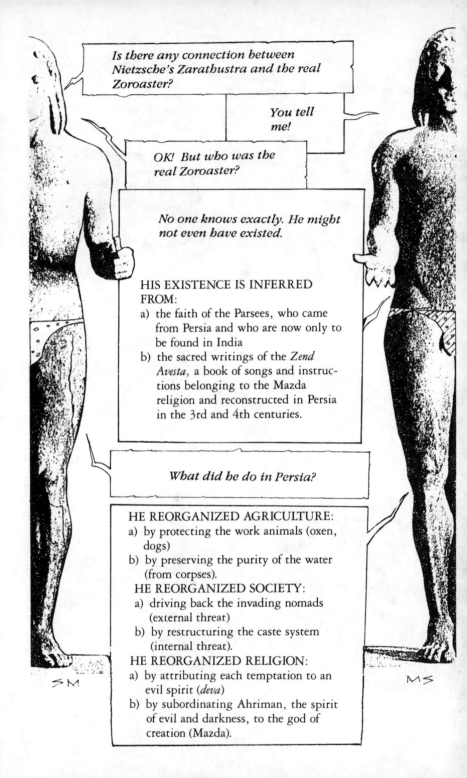

Is there any connection between Nietzsche's Zarathustra and the real Zoroaster?

You tell me!

OK! But who was the real Zoroaster?

No one knows exactly. He might not even have existed.

HIS EXISTENCE IS INFERRED FROM:
a) the faith of the Parsees, who came from Persia and who are now only to be found in India
b) the sacred writings of the *Zend Avesta,* a book of songs and instructions belonging to the Mazda religion and reconstructed in Persia in the 3rd and 4th centuries.

What did he do in Persia?

HE REORGANIZED AGRICULTURE:
a) by protecting the work animals (oxen, dogs)
b) by preserving the purity of the water (from corpses).

HE REORGANIZED SOCIETY:
a) driving back the invading nomads (external threat)
b) by restructuring the caste system (internal threat).

HE REORGANIZED RELIGION:
a) by attributing each temptation to an evil spirit (*deva*)
b) by subordinating Ahriman, the spirit of evil and darkness, to the god of creation (Mazda).

Why did Nietzsche adopt him?

There are two reasons:
2) German philologists were taking a growing interest in the Zenda Avesta
6) Wagner claimed that his <u>Parsifal</u> was linked to the tradition of Zoroaster.

PARSI-FAL = foolish Parsee.

We'll see which one passes.

But the competition was to be a posthumous one since . . .

Wagner died on 13 February 1883 . . .

So, like his Zarathustra, Nietzsche was alone again, with no hope of changing the course of history in his lifetime . . .

Gast
(1854 - 1918)

is a splendid secretary! He takes care of everything!

The only person who stuck by him was a musician, Heinrich Köselitz, a former student from Basle. Nietzsche renamed him Peter Gast, and employed him constantly to transcribe his work.

No hope for the modern world!
Certainly, in the company of the poet Heinrich von
Stein in Nice or Princess Manzuroff in Sils Maria,
Nietzsche moved in 'high society'.
But such society was sterile!

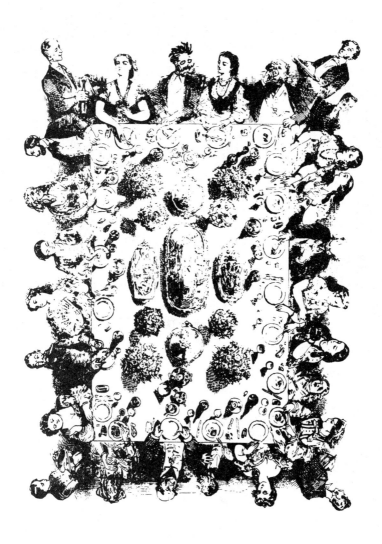

However...

Thus Spoke Zarathustra continued to pose problems . . .

Dear Friend, I can understand why you hide behind this legendary Persian character. BUT . . .

   . . . what do you mean by?:
- a) 'the coming of the last man'?
  Some kind of historical analysis?
- b) 'the Superman'?
  Is this all men together?
  Future man?
- c) 'the hardness' needed for the Superman?

What are its political and practical implications? Finally, the 'eternal recurrence'? Is one really supposed to believe in it? Has it got a scientific basis?

I'm sending you latest book, <u>Beyond Good and Evil</u> by express mail. It says the same thing as my <u>Zarathustra</u>, but in a completely different way.

144

THE LAST MAN

He is the mass of the workers, the bourgeoisie, even the aristocracy, levelled down by democracy and (soon) socialism.

HE IS THE RESULT OF NIHILISM; the result of

- the disappearance of hierarchies
- the levelling of society
- the predominance of materialism.

BEYOND GOOD AND EVIL makes the equation:
RELIGION'
(equality before God)
+ MORALITY
(equality under the law)
+ SCIENCE
(equality in truth)
= the dwarfing of man.

THE SUPERMAN

He represents the higher stage of humanity, but LISTEN! This stage is only reached when the masses are sacrificed to the élite!

If you don't believe me, turn to Chapter 9 of <u>Beyond Good and Evil</u>, *entitled 'What is the Aristocracy?'*

In other words, the *sine qua non* of the Superman's existence is man's exploitation of man.

STRENGTH

This is the law of a 'healthy' society.
Society is sick when it submits to the ideas of the 'dignity of man'
and the 'dignity of work.' Such ideals are the poisoned fruit of cow-
ardliness towards life and its cruelty.

THE ETERNAL RECURRENCE

Contrary to all expectations, *Beyond Good and Evil* does not mention it.

faithless man!

Why this silence? My answer: because Nietzsche had given up trying to justify his new doctrine rationally and was attempting the great leap towards irrationality. Rather than confront the rigours of science, he threw himself into esotericism. With *Human, All-Too-Human* he came close to rationalism—with *Zarathustra* he played with it: a dangerous step.

What could he do?

but then... **Que faire?**

...except prophecy?

It was not a question of halting the wheel of History. But if History is really a wheel and if modern nihilism can be compared to Christianity, if the modern world is a repetition of the Roman world, then . . . after the triumph of the 'new Christianity' there'll be a return to the Middle Ages!!

In the meantime Nietzsche began a revision of his work, and wrote a series of new prefaces and the fifth volume of *The Gay Science*.

Did Nietzsche have an audience?

BOOK FAIR
Leipzig '86

If you have a copy left after the exhibition will you keep it for me?

Ha! Ha! very funny!

The *Communist Party Manifesto* sold like hot cakes despite the anti-socialist law (the third edition was printed clandestinely in Zürich).

Only 114 copies of *Beyond Good and Evil* were sold in six months (printed at the author's cost in Leipzig).

LACKING A PUBLIC, NIETZSCHE FOUND HIM-SELF A SOUL MATE IN DOSTOEVSKY (1821–1881), who had recently died. In Dostoevsky, as in Stendhal, he recognized an aristocratic instinct. In the *The House of the Dead* what stands out is the gulf separating the nobility from the common people, even in their closest relations.

Turgenev was the first to use the NIHILIST in a novel of 1861.

. . . and the revolution will begin in Russia!

THE REVOLUTION? IN 1887 WAR IS AGAIN IMMINENT. IF THE TSAR EMBARKS ON A WAR AND IS DEFEATED, REVOLUTION WILL BE INEV TABLE IN RUSSIA! AND PERHAPS IN GERMANY TOO?

February 1887–Reichstag elections. The Social Democratic Party wins 763,128 votes (it won 100,000 in 1871 and 500,000 in 1877).

In London Mr. Engels has told our special envoy:

Our movement is making splendid progress!

Will France declare War? General Boulanger appears to be set on it!

Kanzler says he can mobilize two million men.

At this historic moment, Nietzsche wrote a sequel to *Beyond Good and Evil* to show how this point had been reached:

The Genealogy of Morals

In it he acknowledges his debt to Paul Rée, then sets out to show that his ideas are in fact the complete opposite of Rée's in their analysis of the 'progress of history.'

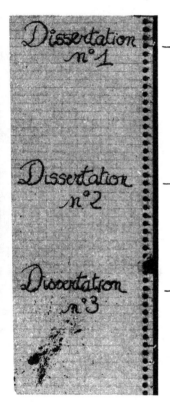

— *Where do the terms 'good' and 'bad' come from?*

From the nobility, the warrior aristocrats. Their meanings have been reversed (initially by the Jews) for the benefit of the people. Since then, the masters have been disposed of, the morality of the common man has won (Chapter 9). And thus began the historic defeat of the nobility, of the 'splendid blond beast' (Chapter 11).

— *How were the lords of the earth defeated?*

They surrendered to their 'guilty conscience'! By humanizing themselves, the nobility submitted to the working class (Chapter 16).

— *Is this reversal of values permanent?*

The victory of the working class was achieved through the preachers. Because the 'weak' cannot triumph over the 'strong' except in groups. And it was the priests who created these groups. But the priests' success is due to the happiness they promise and the example they provide. Now their promise is worthless and their example deathly . . .

I've got a question too: when is breaking time?

So, with everything against him, Nietzsche continued his fight against modern ideas. He was considering a major work which would *bring down the new idols . . .*

A new idol: DARWIN

The recent appearance of Darwin's theory of evolution had upset modern ideas based on Christian morality. This theory justified the victory of the strong over the weak in the struggle for existence. But is it true that the strong always come out on top? The historical defeat of the nobility (the strong) by the working class (the weak) proves the opposite!

The supreme idol: *WAGNER*

In spring 1888 in Turin, Nietzsche was in good spirits. The air suited him and he felt revived by the city's aristocratic atmosphere. The opera *Carmen,* which he had discovered seven years earlier, continued to fascinate him . . .

An opportunity to settle scores. . . . .

'Oh, this old magician! What a clever rattlesnake. The artist of decadence. Is Wagner a man at all? Is he not rather a disease? Corrupter of music! A typical decadent! The worm of the Empire!'

'One pays dearly for having been a follower of Wagner. The old robber! . . . Every year processions of the finest young men and maidens are led into his labyrinth that he may swallow them up.'

Having unburdened himself, Nietzsche decided to publish separately his *Revaluation of All Values,* from which he developed:

TWIGHLIGHT OF THE IDOLS

What's the use of reason? Ring out the cracked sound of the revered idols: A hammer blow to Greek wisdom!

Reality behind Appearance, happiness through virtue, the truth that lies in reason, not in essence.

How hollow it all sounds!

SOCRATES

A hammer-blow to Christianity . . . and a broken cry escapes from the poor in spirit, a thin sigh from the will-less—the sick.

By poisoning the Germans, the Catholic Church has made these sick ones masters over all . . .

. . . But in the end the church became too expensive for the new masters. So I invented a cheap Church for them, a Church with no pope, nor hierarchy, no pomp.

And no indulgences either, eh?

Martinuf Lutheruf

1888

A year of mourning for the Reich: the emperor Wilhelm I died in March; his successor Friedrich III died after three months on the throne. Wilhelm II inherits the throne at 29.

It was a year of exceptional productivity for Nietzsche.
After:
THE CASE OF WAGNER
and
TWILIGHT OF THE IDOLS
came
THE ANTI-CHRIST.

All these developed out of work intended for the Will to Power, which Nietzsche abandoned.

With *The Anti-Christ*, Nietzsche launched into an attack on another star:

> Nevertheless, my dear Nietzsche, if you read his <u>Intellectual and Moral Reform</u> *(1871) you will se that you have many things in common!*

> Yes, I know: we both feel nostalgic for the German people, about hierarchies and castes, and both dislike socialists and democracy, but still. . .

Ernest Renan

(1823—1893) Specialist in the history of religions Famous for his LIFE OF JESUS.

J. Kaftan
Theologian.
1848 - 1927

. . . but what makes you think that Jesus was a genius?
— Christianity started off as an uprising against the 'good'
and the 'just' (i.e. the aristocracy, their privileges and their
ordering of society).

This is all Paul's fault! He was the one who invented Christianity!

Come along, Paul, we know it was you! You'd do better to own up...

OK, I confess: I was the one who took Jesus away from the cave. If it hadn't been for me, he'd be dead as a doornail! You should've seen the chaos when they started hunting down the first disciples!...

What happened?

Hang on!

Why did the idiot have to get involved?

...At the beginning I was well in with the Pharisees... but I wouldn't have got to be boss with them. And the Christians had just lost theirs... A golden opportunity!...

...After all, perhaps HE was the Messiah! Reading the texts, I realized that it might stick, but on one condition: that if he came to atone for original sin, then we'd be even more indebted to God. Good news, wouldn't you say?

There was only one Christian and he died on the cross. And here's what the rest deserve:

LAW AGAINST CHRISTIANITY.

Proclaimed on the Day of Redemption, the first day of Year One (30 September 1888 of the false calendar)

Article 1 – Anything which is against nature is a vice. The most decadent type of man is the priest: he *teaches* against nature. You cannot reason with a priest; the only course is to imprison him.

Article 2 – Holding holy office is an attack on public morality. The sentence will be more severe for a Protestant than for a Catholic, and more severe for a liberal Protestant than for a puritan. The closer one gets to science, the greater is the crime of being a Christian. The greatest of all criminals is therefore the *philosopher*.

Article 3 – The loathesome place where Christianity hatched its monstrous eggs will be razed to the ground, and being the most *sacrilegious* place on earth it will be the terror of future generations. Poisonous snakes will be bred there.

The Anti-Christ

165

... and where do women fit in all this?

It was man's thoughtfulness and consideration for women that found expression in the Church decree: *mulier taceat in ecclesia!* It was for women's good when Napoleon gave the all too eloquent Madame de Staël to understand *mulier taceat* in politicis! And I think it is a real friend of women that counsels them today: *mulier taceat de muliere!*

Nietzsche loves women with character—like Carmen—as long as they die in the end.

5 th movement

At that time, Nietzsche was trying to attract the maximum amount of attention, convinced that he was a historic moment in history!

Was this sheer megalomania?
His philosophy had been the theme
of conferences in Copenhagen since
February . . .

It's only since I came on the scene that there have been great politics!

With *Ecce Homo* Nietzsche did publicly what Brandes had asked him to do privately: He formally presented himself – his life, his work and his aspirations.

The tragedy began! Nietzsche envisaged that the first edition of *The Anti-Christ* would run to a million copies in seven languages. He was not to get to see a single one. He just had time to send messages to friends and a publication note to all the university courses in Europe!

God's on Earth! Can't you see how the heavens are rejoicing? I've taken possession of my kingdom. I'm throwing the Pope into prison and I'm having Bismark, Wilhelm and Stoecker executed!

Adolf Stoecker (1835–1909), Protestant preacher in Berlin. Founder of the Party for Christian Socialism in 1878.

171

On 3 January 1889, in the Piazza Carlo Alberto, Nietzsche saw a coachman beating his horse. He rushed forward and then collapsed! . . .

His landlord took him home.
His friend Franz Overbeck* arrived from Basle.
Nietzsche acted the fool all night!

* Franz Overbeck (1837–1905), professor of Church History at Basle University, a faithful friend of Nietzsche since 1870.

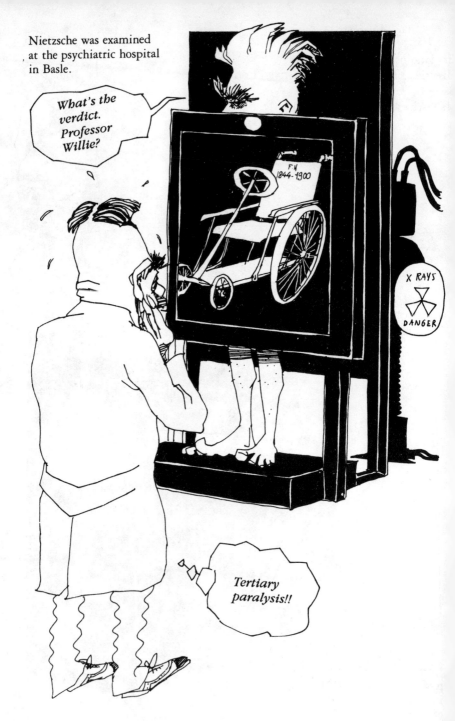

He was transferred to the University clinic at Jena near his family home . . . Diagnosis, please?:

From May 1890, for seven years his mother nursed him in Naumburg.

The Ruhr miners' strike

- Authorization of socialist activity
- Founding of the Second International
- Resignation of Bismarck
- Franco-Russian alliance
- Intensification of national conflicts
- Out and out militarism
- Advent of nihilism
- Downfall of the German aristocracy
- The death of God . . .
    . . . none of which is of any interest to
    Nietzsche any more!

Still . . . at night . . . perhaps . . .

178

179

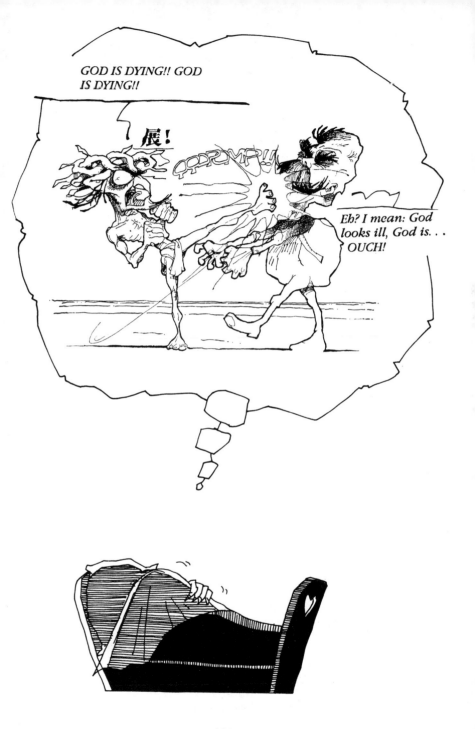

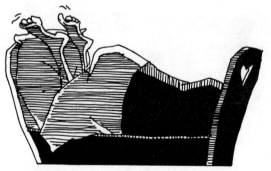

When his mother died Nietzsche's
sister Elisabeth took charge of him,
moving in with him and his 'archives'
in Weimar.

As the heir to her brother's work, Elisabeth arranged for the publication of his complete works.

Thus appeared the book which Nietzsche had abandoned: *The Will to Power* (developed from various notes and rough drafts).

Elisabeth's bright idea was to pretend that letters written by her brother to some close friend (Overbeck, for example) were in fact addressed to her. In this way she was able to make people believe that she was completely in her brother's confidence with regard to his work.

This was the beginning of fame!
He was visited on his death bed, swathed in white, and almost completely
paralysed . . .

Friedrich Nietzsche died on

AUG. 25,
1900.

From 1903 onwards, Nietzsche was ranked with the famous! Soon, numerous groups, belonging to widely different tendencies, started calling themselves Nietzschian.

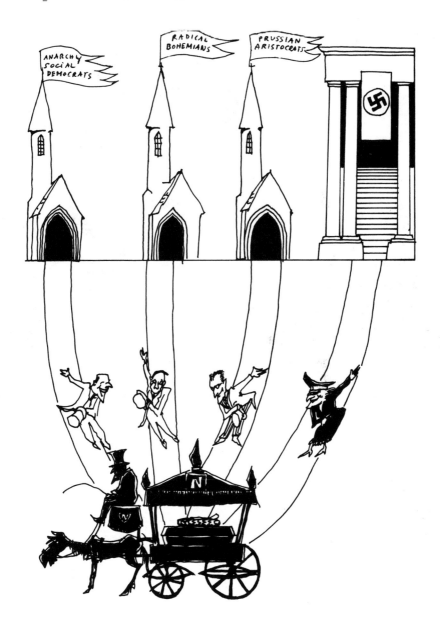

One of his better-known followers was Adolf!

It started with Bernhardt Föster, husband of "Lama", and doctor of philosophy. He was a notorious anti-semite and a militant committed to German imperialism. After the defeat of 1918, the German bourgeoisie used every means at its disposal to achieve its end. In the face of the socialist threat and democratic impotence, it did everything in its power to attract the support of the petite bourgeoisie.

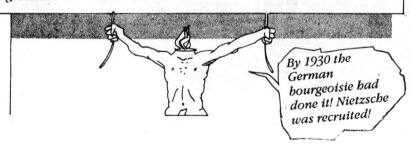

By 1930 the German bourgeoisie had done it! Nietzsche was recruited!

The price of all this involuntary glory was that Nietzsche's name was cited at the Nurembourg Trials of the great war criminals on 17 January 1946.

'His vision of the masses being governed without constraints by the rulers presaged the Nazi regime. Nietzsche believed in the supreme race and the primacy of Germany in which he saw a young soul and inexhaustible reserves.'

In 1956 Lukacs drove the final nail into the coffin of 'Nietzschian pre-Fascism.' In spite of Albert Camus, Nietzsche then faced a period in the desert of obscurity . . .

. . . *until the 1960s, since when his ghost; s has haunted Europe. . .*

. . . and school textbooks!

APPENDICES

Glossary of Nietszchean Terms

THEOLOGY: science of divine revelation

PHILOLOGY: study of the authenticity of texts

PHILOSOPHY: critique of prejudices

EPISTEMOLOGY: science of knowledge

APPEARANCE: product of the senses and of knowledge

BEING: that which is on this side of appearance

TRAGIC CHORUS: interpreter of the pain of living

WILL: being, according to Schopenhauer

GERMAN SPIRIT: traditional courage of the German people towards the cruelty of existence

STOICISM: individual courage (invented by the Greeks) towards the cruelty of existence

DEATH OF GOD: fruit of theology and philology

THERMODYNAMICS: study of the transformations of heat

ETERNAL RECURRENCE: Stoic thesis on the evolution of the cosmos

NIHILISM: levelling tendency

LAST MAN: result of nihilism

SUPERMAN: first victim of nihilism – he will return!

DEMOCRACY: means of nihilism

SOCIALISM: aim of nihilism

CHRISTIANITY: name of nihilism under the Roman Empire—it poisoned the Germans

Nietzsche	Books published		
born in saxony			1844
his father dies			
discovers Schopenhauer	philological works		1866
meets Wagner			
is appointed at Basle			
lectures on Greek tragedy			
	The Birth of Tragedy		1871
lectures on education			
	Thoughts out of Season	1	1873
		2–3	1874
Bayreuth festival		4	1876
stay at Naples	*Human, All-Too-Human*		1878
gives up teaching	*Assorted Opinions and Maxims*		1879
	The Wanderer and his Shadow		
	Aurora [or the Dawn]: Thoughts on		
	Moral Prejudices		1881
conceives the idea of Eternal	*The Gay Science*		1882
Recurrence			
falls in love with Lou von			
Salomé			
death of Wagner	*Thus Spoke Zarathustra*	1–2	1883
(and of Marx)		3	1884
		4	1885
	The Good and Evil		1886
	The Genealogy of Morals		1887
Brandes lectures on him	*The Case of Wagner*		1888
	Twilight of the Idols		
collapses in Turin	*The Anti-Christ*		1889
	Ecce Homo		
	Nietzsche Against Wagner		
	The Dionysos Dithyrambs		
death in Weimar			1900